EL SALVADOR

MTK

EL SALVADOR

PHOTOGRAPHS BY ADAM KUFELD

INTRODUCTION BY ARNOLDO RAMOS • POETRY BY MANLIO ARGUETA

W • W • NORTON & COMPANY • NEW YORK • LONDON

Printed in Italy.

The text of this book is composed in New Aster,
with the display set in Berkeley Bold.
Composition by Trufont Typographers, Inc.
Manufacturing by American Pizzi Offset Corporation.
Book design by Candace Maté.

Translations of poetry by Jennifer Manriquez and Stacey Ross.

First Edition

Library of Congress Cataloging-in-Publication Data
Kufeld, Adam.
    El Salvador / photographs by Adam Kufeld ; introduction by Arnoldo
  Ramos ; poetry by Manlio Argueta.
       p.   cm.
     1. El Salvador—Politics and government—1979– —Pictorial works.
  2. El Salvador—Description and travel—1981– —Views.   3. El
  Salvador—Poetry. I. Argueta, Manlio, 1936–   II. Title.
  F1488.3.K84   1990   972.8405′3—dc20   90-42203

ISBN 0-393-02811-9
ISBN 0-393-30645-3 (pbk)

W.W. Norton & Company, Inc., 500 Fifth Avenue, New York, N.Y. 10110
W.W. Norton & Company, Ltd., 10 Coptic Street, London WC1A 1PU

1 2 3 4 5 6 7 8 9 0

CONTENTS

INTRODUCTION
BY ARNOLDO RAMOS

*B*efore the arrival of the Spaniards, the Pipil called their land Cuzcatlan, in the Nahuatl language the "land of richness." Natural and social disasters had forced the Pipil to migrate from the steppes of northern Mexico to the Central American isthmus in search of a promised land. Cuzcatlan's richness and beauty surpassed all expectations. Here was a land of eternal spring, lavished with densely forested valleys and fertile volcanic soils and endowed by one of nature's most generous water systems. Mighty rivers embraced in their silvery arms the width and length of the richest valleys imaginable. Emerald lagoons reflected in their pure waters the blue cones of smoking volcanoes.

For thousands of years, Cuzcatlan was the mother who had generously provided roofs, clothing, medicines, game, fish, corn, cocoa, and vegetables to hundreds of generations of her children: Pipil, Lenca, Pokoman. Economic and social life in Cuzcatlan revolved around the generosity of the land and man's free access to her riches. As historian David Browning writes,

> The concept of the community of man with the soil, weather and plants was the basis of attitudes towards the use and ownership of land. To the Indian, private and individual ownership of land was as meaningless as private ownership of the sky, the weather, or the sea. Land, like the plants that grew on it, was for man's use and could not be claimed under exclusive individual ownership.[1]

The Spaniards changed Cuzcatlan's name and fate. Today Cuzcatlan is known as El Salvador, the Saviour, and the Pipil's paradise has been turned into one of the worst social and ecological disasters in the Americas. Two percent of El Salvador's population now own 60 percent of all real estate and grow crops—mainly coffee, cotton, sugar—not for feeding their fellow human beings but for fully privatized exports to foreign markets. Both the scandalous concentration of economic and political power in the hands of an elite and the militarization of state power has resulted in a decade-long civil war. One third of the five million population has been displaced from their homes, and more than seventy thousand people have died, mostly at the hands of official forces.

To finance a war that rages across a landscape the size of Massachusetts, each day the U.S. government sends the right-wing government and the military more than $1.3 million in aid. Intensive air bombings, forest fires, and "scorched earth" military campaigns have effectively combined with the disastrous effects of an unrestrained agro-export economy threatening to extinguish the last signs of life of a dying environment.

According to a Green Paper issued by the Environmental Project on Central America (EPOCA), "Virtually every ecosystem in El Salvador is in ruins. The country's once dense forest cover has all but disappeared. Dust bowls and denuded hillsides have replaced lush valleys." As a result, harvests have dwindled and water supplies are diminishing in a country where nine in ten people do not have access to safe drinking water and one in four children is malnourished.

Because pesticides as well as waste from industry and coffee production flow untreated into the water habitats, the EPOCA report says, "every major watershed and river basin is degraded." This includes the huge Lempa River, the single largest watershed in all of Central America. Citing a report from the United Nations Food and Agriculture Organization, the Green Paper concludes that the tropical country is undergoing a process of "desertification."

The case of El Salvador confirms a very sad truth: when it comes to negative power, human beings seem omnipotent. We can turn a tropical garden into a desert, a social paradise into a hellish nightmare. We can destroy an entire country—in the phrase made infamous by an American officer during the Vietnam War—"in order to save it," for what we subjectively define as the interests of our country, class, or party.

Today, we—Salvadorans and North Americans—have been given a chance to prove that we can also use power constructively. After ten years of living in what we must describe as apocalyptic times—under the sign of war, pestilence, and utter destruction—the prospects of peace and reconstruction have appeared. In the wake of the end of the Cold War, the Salvadoran government and the Farabundo Martí Front for National Liberation (FMLN) signed in April 1990, under the auspices of the United Nations, what could become a workable and reasonable format for forging peace through a process of demilitarization and democratization.

A national consensus for peace is growing in both El Salvador and the United States. After a powerful rebel military offensive and horrible war crimes committed by the Salvadoran military, important individuals belonging to the government and the business sector, some army officers, and, very importantly, the Bush administration have finally come to accept a negotiated political solution, not the escalation of military activities, as the only possible means of ending the war. Thus, with the exception of key army officers who find war very profitable and fear that peace would bring about their political and social displacement, the rest of Salvadoran society is ready to be mobilized for peace, demilitarization-democratization, and reconstruction.

To succeed in this gigantic task, Salvadorans

have to overcome decades of social, political, and economic polarization and build from the ashes of war and, for the first time in our history, a national consensus.

We—and all those interested in helping us forge a new reality—must also come to terms with the root causes of our war. The following pages offer an account of the Salvadoran conflict that points to the Salvadoran state as the principal source of social conflict. In fact, given the authoritarian and militaristic history of the state institutions, peace and democracy simply do not have a future unless the old state is democratized and demilitarized.

THE NATION-ESTATE: 1880s TO 1932

The birth of Salvadoran society was marked by war, genocide, and enslavement of the population. First, the Spanish conquerors used rape, pillage, and widespread massacres to subdue the Pipil and possess their lands. Then, the Crown proceeded to institutionalize the private ownership of land and human beings, awarding the victors huge allotments of land and supplying Indian labor by means of *encomiendas*: Indians were literally "recommended" into the charge of a Spaniard who was responsible for their conversion to Christianity and who could receive tribute or work from them in his estate.

Established as feudal lords over the Indian and mestizo population, the *encomenderos* undertook the first steps to convert a country that had not known private property into a privately owned estate. By the late sixteenth century, they began to turn their lands into privatized commercial estates. The first cash crop exported to metropolitan markets was indigo, a natural dye in great demand in the European textile industry.

Meanwhile, the progressive ideas and extraordinary success of the liberal revolution in the United States inspired a generation of patriots with dreams of another Eldorado in Central America:

> The States of the Isthmus from Panama to Guatemala will perhaps form a confederation. This magnificent location between the great oceans could in time become the emporium of the world. Its canals will shorten the distances throughout the world, strengthen commercial ties with Europe, America, Asia, and bring that happy region tribute from the four quarters of the globe. Perhaps some day the capital of the world may be located there, just as Constantine claimed Byzantium was the capital of the ancient world.[2]

This spirited version of the Central American liberal project was written in 1815 by Latin America's greatest—and must frustrated—nation-builder, Simón Bolívar.

From the second to the fourth decades of the nineteenth century, local liberals fought and lost a series of wars against the *encomendero* establishment in an effort to construct a modern nation-state capable of consolidating the isthmus' newly won independence from Spain. The liberal dreamers were led by the patriot Francisco Morazan and envisioned a federated republic, sovereign, economically self-sufficient, and ruled by republican institutions comparable to those which had guaranteed the success of the United States.

Morazan's project for an integrated and self-sufficient Central America lacked an economic base. At that time, the principal source of power resided in the land, and those who possessed it were to remain to this day adamantly opposed to the political ideals of liberalism. When the fierce opposition of the reactionary landed sectors combined with the interests of England and the United States to construct a canal through the isthmus, the liberal dream of modernization collapsed. Central America was turned into the present nightmare of five pseudo-republics, condemned to constant internal turmoil and perpetual economic dependence on external powers.

U.S. policy was originally supportive of revolutionary change in Central America. Contrary to future assertions, the famous 1823 document drafted by John Quincy Adams and James Monroe and known as the Monroe Doctrine, welcomed revolutions in Latin America and pledged that the United States would not become involved in them. By the 1890s, however, U.S. policy had turned openly counterrevolutionary. "Manifest destiny," the drive to become the world's most powerful nation, converted the Caribbean–Central American region into the United States'

"backyard," an exclusive zone for economic, political, and military operations. From then on, Central America would become "geopolitically" strategic for the growing North American empire.

In the 1880s, the cultivation and export of coffee—not the canal, as the liberals had wished—linked El Salvador and the rest of Central America to the world—the world market, that is. Instead of building a modern nation-state, coffee facilitated the transformation of the old colonial hacienda into the nation-estate that we know today.

The proverbial "fourteen families" that came to concentrate most of the arable land in their estates thrived in a new state apparatus that first outlawed all communally held property and then promoted the privatization of the lands best suited for the cultivation of the new cash crop. Coffee agriculture and its encroachment onto the best lands began to displace subsistence agriculture and reduce food production for the internal market. Land expropriations and strictly enforced antivagrancy laws soon turned the peasant population into the servants, peons, and urban wage laborers of the landed few.

The transfer from indigo to coffee, from colonial to neocolonial dependence, was carried out by the direct descendants of the *encomendero* families—the original nucleus of the Salvadoran landed oligarchy. Their names were Alfaro, Regalado, Dueñas, Palomo, Escalon, Orellana, Prado, and Melendez. Subsequently, a new generation of immigrant coffee planters added their names to the list: Alvarez Bloom, Canessa, Daglio, D'Aubuisson, De Sola, Deininger, Duke, Freund, Hill, Sol Millet, and Wright. That these names resonate today with the same intensity as they did one hundred years ago offers more than ample testimony to the fossilized nature of Salvadoran society.

By monopolizing the land, foreign trade, and the state apparatus, the Salvadoran oligarchy institutionalized the polarization of society into two distinct social and economic classes—the haves and the have-nots, the dominators and the dominated. This economic, social, and political polarization, acting in conjunction with the United States' interpretation of the Monroe Doctrine as "Central America for the North Americans," set the stage for the Salvadoran conflagrations of the twentieth century.

THE MILITARY STATE: 1932–1979

The crash of 1929 and the subsequent worldwide depression brought about the collapse of the coffee economy in El Salvador. In 1932, starving peasants, artisans, and workers, armed only with machetes and stones, rebelled against their misery. A fledgling Communist party attempted fruitlessly to channel the social explosion into the formation of a more progressive state. The coffee barons, who for the first two decades of the twentieth century had ruled the state through the dic-tatorship of the Melendez–Quinones clan, had the clear option of implementing economic reforms and democratic measures or of responding with repression.

The choice was genocide. The actual uprising lasted a few days and was easily defeated. The state's repressive forces did not need the assistance of uninvited U.S. marines waiting on their ships off the port of Acajutla. But the sheer nightmare that followed the aborted uprising shaped the psyche of every Salvadoran born after 1932 and sealed the nation's future fate. Within a month of the rebellion, 30,000 Salvadoran peasants, workers, women, and children were assassinated in cold blood by the army and paramilitary groups organized by the coffee barons. The army and the oligarchy sought to teach a lesson that would never be forgotten. And they succeeded. In 1980, after having assimilated the historical shock of 1932, Salvadoran peasants and workers would name their revolutionary vanguard after the man who attempted to lead the first challenge to the oligarchic state, Farabundo Marti.

The massacre of 30,000 Salvadorans froze the fires of class conflict and bought the powers that be nearly half a century of "peace and stability." However, in order to defend their monopoly over the country's wealth, the landed oligarchy had to accommodate the interests of the military. In the ensuing division of labor, the military run the affairs of the state and the oligarchy those of business.

11

From 1932 to 1979 the Salvadoran state was a military dictatorship. After the overthrow of General Maximiliano Hernandez Martinez (1932–1944), absolute power moved from the hands of a single dictator to those of a clique of military officers—the successive graduating classes, known as *tandas*, of the Military Academy. Growing demands by the population for democratization were met by rigged elections guaranteeing the victory of the officer selected by the *tanda* in power.

As the military began to institutionalize their power and turn into society's most powerful group, the oligarchy expanded and diversified the economy. Sugar and cotton were added to the export list, pushing more and more peasants off their lands. Foreign trade and all banking operations were virtually privatized. Expansion plus diversification, in conjunction with external stimuli from U.S. investors, created conditions for an initial phase of industrialization.

The division of labor between the oligarchy and the military worked most effectively until the 1960s, when the fruits of success and the rapid rate of growth brought the system's contradictions to the surface. Faced with a structural crisis, the agro-export establishment ignored all internal and external pressures for economic change and democratization. As in 1932, the powers that be resorted to the only medicine they knew, repression and genocide. By 1979–80, the crisis had turned into full-scale civil war. The chain of events leading to this social catastrophe had begun in the 1960s, a time of radical change throughout Latin America.

The Economic Crisis

In the 1960s, the impact of the Cuban revolution jolted the Central American states out of their complacency. With the exception of Costa Rica, where a process of social reforms and democratization had been under way since the late 1940s, the remaining countries were living under military dictatorships similar to the one overthrown by the Cuban revolutionaries in 1959 with tactics of guerrilla warfare and popular insurrection. In addition, the region's plantation economies, virtually unchanged since the 1880s, entered a stage of structural crisis from which they were never to recover.

Convinced of the impossibility of implementing change by peaceful means alone, Nicaraguan and Guatemalan youth organized the first guerrilla foci in the mountains of their respective countries. Salvadoran workers, peasants, and students increased their levels of organization and started to debate the option of armed struggle. Consequently, the vision of new Cubas arising from the ashes of outdated militarized states began to haunt U.S. policy.

Washington responded with a two-track strategy. On one hand, it offered a development program, known as the Alliance for Progress, intended to reform and modernize the region's backward forms of capitalist development. The program contained plans for a first phase of industrialization and the integration of the region's economies into a Central American Common Market. It also called for a series of social and economic reforms to offset the spread of revolutionary alternatives: the development of public housing, health and hygiene programs, proper compensation for workers, the eradication of illiteracy, fairer tax laws, and above all, agrarian reform. Unfortunately, the U.S. package emphasized security over social reforms. Alliance for Progress came accompanied by intensive counterinsurgency training programs for the area's security forces, a much more active role for the CIA, and the formation of the Central American Defense Council (CONDECA). CONDECA, the military counterpart of the Common Market, sought the modernization of the region's armies as well as their integration into a single body capable of ending "the communist threat" in the region.

The Salvadoran military welcomed Washington's counterinsurgency package. From then on, U.S. policy's obsession with containing "communism" in El Salvador became the armed forces' chief source of income and power as well as the justification for gross human rights violations. U.S. military aid was soon translated into a stronger and more efficient repressive apparatus. CIA expertise resulted in the formation of new army intelligence units, which would engender, in turn, paramilitary death-squad entities like the Nationalist Democratic Organization (ORDEN) and the future politicans of the country, such as Carlos Humberto Romero and Roberto D'Aubuisson. On the other hand, the U.S. plan for modernization through reforms created a permanent structural division within the Salvadoran oligarchy.

In the 1950s, a sector of the oligarchy had branched out from agriculture into marketing and finance and now saw the need for industrialization. This modernizing group maintained that wealth, formerly generated and concentrated in the agro-export sector, had to be distributed to create a market for industrial goods. Taxes had to be raised to finance the required infrastructure. Revolutionary tendencies had to be quelled by repression accompanied by superficial reforms. But the ancestral oligarchy categorically opposed any structural change that would undermine its hegemony over the export economy and the security apparatus.

In the early 1960s, U.S. government pressures and the enticement of private investors forced a compromise among the competing sectors of the ruling elite. Industrialization was given the green light, provided it would not lead to the emergence of an entrepreneurial class capable of challenging the landed oligarchy and pressing for an expansion of the internal market through redistribution of wealth. If Salvadorans could not afford to

13

buy the products manufactured by their own labor, markets could be found abroad. But social reforms, especially any transformation of the land tenure structures, were not to be permitted under any circumstances. The compromise demonstrated both the near omnipotence of the landed oligarchy and the fact that, for U.S. interests, profit was a more important concern than reforms.

Thus, El Salvador did undergo a process of semi-industrialization, but without changing its basic economic, social, and political structures. In the 1960s and 1970s, the economy expanded considerably, first within the framework of the Central American Common Market and, after its demise, by attracting foreign capital (garment and electronics plants) with tax incentives, free-trade zones, and cheap labor. But the expansion proved unviable, economically and politically.

World market prices for coffee, cotton, and sugar began to plunge in the mid-1960s, at the same time that the costs of imports kept going up. In addition, the industrial activity assigned to El Salvador consisted of assembling, finishing, and packaging consumer goods (textiles, footwear, beverages) that were partially processed abroad. It still required the importation of the products to be processed, and of course, of capital. Foreign capital ended up dominating the industrial sector, with its advanced technology and the scale of its organization and operations. "Industrialization" was never designed to break

the circle of dependence on foreign markets and investors. Foreign capital, especially from the United States, was simply using the country for its extremely cheap and abundant labor.

Political tensions began to rise in direct proportion to the perception by more and more social sectors that the very system that had worked so well for the few had plunged the many into a generalized state of landlessness, unemployment, impoverishment, and extreme exploitation. The subsequent radicalization of the peasantry can be explained by the consequences of the rapid expansion of export agriculture. Following the pattern established in the 1880s, by the end of the 1970s at least 60 percent of rural families had either no land at all or less than subsistence plots. El Salvador's 1971 census showed that 64 percent of the land belonged to 4 percent of the country's farms. Although the agricultural sector generated high demand for rural labor at planting and harvest time—only an average of three months out of the year—low prevailing wages condemned the landless to abject poverty. In 1973 they were earning only $1.10 per day.

Those who escaped the countryside and went to the cities in search of jobs did not fare any better. Despite a rapidly growing manufacturing sector, joblessness had already reached crisis proportions before the outbreak of civil war. At its peak in 1977, manufacturing employed only 59,000 workers, and the average wage never exceeded $2 per day. According to studies of this period, over half of the men who migrated to San Salvador became construction workers, and the majority of the women became domestic servants, prostitutes, or street vendors. Thus, despite the nation's impressive aggregate growth rates in the post-World War II period, the increasing riches of the few represented the growing misery of the many.

The Rise of the Political Opposition

El Salvador's economic growth also produced significant social changes. The size of the working and nonworking classes increased. The state bureaucracy expanded rapidly, and so did the country's tiny middle class of professionals and small merchants. The middle class, caught between the poles of wealth and poverty, began demanding a political voice and economic reforms. These demands soon received active support from new sectors of the Catholic church, which, inspired by the shift toward social activism sanctioned in the Second Vatican Council (1961–62) and the Medellín Conference of Latin American Bishops (1968), had decided to play the role of catalyst for social and political change.

The middle class responded with two political parties that espoused an electoral road to change: the Christian Democratic party (PDC), and the National Revolutionary Movement (MNR), founded in 1960 and 1969, respectively. Because of its anticommunist as well as its anti-oligarchic stand, the PDC became the favorite of U.S. agencies, the Catholic church's Social Christian movement, and the international Christian Democratic movement. Unlike the PDC, the MNR developed a more open stand toward the left. Through its membership in the Socialist International, the worldwide organization of social democracy, this party established excellent international relations that would strengthen its role in future political coalitions.

The left also began to seek new forms of political organization. Conditions were ripe. The slum communities around the capital were swelling with restless refugees from the countryside and from Honduras. Thousands had been expelled from the neighboring country after a bloody war in 1969. The electoral work of the PDC and the MNR, as well as the involvement of the Catholic church and U.S. agencies (the Agency for International Development and the American Institute for Free Labor Development) in organizing urban and rural workers, had helped raise both the expectations and the political consciousness of the popular classes. A general strike staged in 1967, followed by a powerful teachers' strike the next year, also conveyed the clear message that the urban working class was ready for higher levels of organization and militancy.

The first revolutionary organizations of what would become, a decade later, the Farabundo Martí National Liberation Front (FMLN) were born in 1970. The founders, activists from the

Communist party and the Christian Democratic movement, questioned the strategies followed by their respective parties. In their opinion, the electoral road to change would be easily blocked by repression and fraud. They argued that the oligarchy and their military allies could only be defeated by a strategy integrating political and military means of struggle.

The new activists held that their strategy could be executed, first, by creating "mass fronts" in which all oppressed sectors of society could participate and press their immediate economic and political demands; second, by forging a strategic alliance between peasants and workers; and third, on the basis of this seminal convergence, a broader alliance with marginal and middle-class sectors. Finally, to meet the inevitable repression from the state, the popular movement would have to develop its own military instruments of self-defense. The new radical organizations assigned to themselves the task of becoming the political and military brain and backbone of the projected mass movement. Accordingly, they structured themselves as political formations, set out to gain influence in the existing mass movement, and took the first steps toward constituting the nucleus of the future people's army.

The Political Crisis

The breaking point of the political crisis came in 1972, when the rapidly evolving opposition began to challenge the state with two clearly defined paths for change: through the legal and peaceful means of elections; and through the extralegal means of armed struggle and insurrection. Both paths were revolutionary for they sought the construction of a modern, democratic nation-state out of the ruins of the old military nation-estate built in the 1880s and the trauma of 1932.

To challenge forty years of military rule in the 1972 presidential elections, Christian Democrats, social democrats, and the legal arm of the outlawed Communist party formed the broadest political coalition possible at the time, the National Opposition Union. UNO canvassed and raised the political consciousness of the entire population with a platform that is still relevant today: agrarian reform, nationalization of foreign trade and banks, dismantling of the state's repressive apparatus, democratization of the state, and depoliticization of the armed forces and their subordination to civilian rule.

Most observers agreed that UNO candidates, José Napoleón Duarte of the PDC and Guillermo Ungo of the MNR, clearly won the elections. However, since elections were intended to legitimize the oligarchic state, not to end it, the military simply collected all ballot boxes and announced Colonel Arturo Molina's victory. The blatancy and extent of the electoral fraud triggered widespread public protests and even an attempted coup by a group of civilian and military elements. In response, Nicaragua and Guatemala, acting under the aegis of CONDECA and supervised by U.S. advisors, sent troops and planes to check the revolt. For its part, the new government unleashed a wave of repression against the entire opposition. Duarte and other leaders were exiled; the National University was closed for two years; trade union leaders were imprisoned or exiled. Persecution of religious activists and rural workers led to massacres in the countryside.

Much to their credit, the parties that comprised UNO kept alive the electoral means of struggle until another blatant fraud in the elections of 1977 closed all avenues for peaceful change. Although defeated by fraud, UNO's organizing and campaigning contributed greatly to the radicalization of broad sectors of the population.

By blocking all peaceful roads to democratization and persecuting the opposition, the military laid the basis for the armed revolution of the 1980s. Thousands of peasants, workers, and youthful members of the middle class turned to revolutionary alternatives when their expectations for peaceful change were so blatantly aborted by the state. By the mid-1970s, those social sectors which had never been permitted to exercise their political rights—peasants, farmworkers, slum dwellers, street vendors, market women, the unemployed—were joining extralegal unions and constructing their own mass fronts. Formerly organized sectors such as students, teachers, and industrial workers were also joining these unprecedented grass-roots formations. A political front based on the alliance of peasants and workers was now in the making.

The masses, the most powerful and explosive political agent of the country, were on the move. Now that they had their own political instruments, they started to organize and mobilize around concrete demands—higher wages, running water, and the release of their imprisoned comrades. Inevitably, the masses also began to demand the drastic transformation of the recalcitrant state. The Molina government, responding to directives from the modernizing sector of the oligarchy, answered with a dose of repression and a bit of reform. On one hand it revitalized ORDEN and on the other it announced an "agrarian transformation" program that only dared to affect 4 percent of the country's land.

This timid attempt at reformism in the midst of a worsening crisis elicited the wrath of the all-powerful ultra-right. Molina's reform initiative was canceled by the landowning dynasties—the Hills, Llachs, Regalado Dueñas—who proceeded to regain control of the state. General Carlos Humberto Romero, a former head of ORDEN, was chosen as the new candidate for the 1977 presidential elections. After another fraudulent military victory, Romero sought to solve the political crisis by smashing the opposition once and for all.

To protect their interests in this time of crisis,

17

the agro-export oligarchy and their allies in the military entered a phase of political reorganization. Reactionary landowners founded new political organizations such as the Growers Front of the Eastern Region (FARO)—the seminal group that would give birth in 1981 to the Nationalist Republic Alliance party (ARENA). The National Association of Private Enterprise (ANEP) and the Chamber of Commerce, formerly economic organizations, were converted into political fronts and war chests for organizing and financing openly fascist paramilitary death-squad units— the White Warriors Union (UGB), the Anti-Communist Armed Forces of Liberation–War of Elimination (FALANGE).

The excesses of the Romero administration detonated the inevitable social explosion. During the first months of 1979, the government killed 406 people and declared open war on the Catholic church, trade unions, and the universities. But massacres, mass arrests, and widespread tortures in both the cities and the countryside failed to paralyze the popular movement. On the contrary, repression multiplied membership in the mass popular fronts and convinced their members that armed struggle was the most effective instrument for self-defense and for the ultimate overthrow of the regime.

By the time the Sandinista revolutionaries were entering Managua in July 1979, foreign capital had already run away from El Salvador and the government was completely isolated. The Carter administration and the Archbishop of San Salvador were among the regime's most powerful critics. Concerned policymakers in Washington began to see El Salvador as "another Nicaragua" in the making.

THE COUNTERINSURGENCY STATE: 1979–1990

In October 1979, a coup staged by young military officers overthrew the Romero government. To prevent another successful Central American revolution, which would alter the face of the region, U.S. policymakers decided to convert the Salvadoran military state into a counterinsurgency war state.

The political component of the U.S. counterinsurgency policy sought to defeat the revolution by institutionalizing from above a centrist-reformist model—a project that would end the polarizing policies of the ultra-right as well as deprive the revolution of its huge social base by implementing a series of structural reforms in the economic and political spheres. Accordingly, a "revolutionary" junta was established in late October constituting a civilian-military government. The junta was made up by members of the UNO coalition (Christian Democrats, social democrats, and the electoral left) and reform-oriented sectors of the military acceptable to the Pentagon and the modernizing oligarchy. The new political formula also adopted key elements from the old UNO platform—redistribution of land on a large scale, nationalization of banks and foreign trade, and a campaign of national reconciliation—presenting them as the foundation of its social and economic "revolution."

But Washington's efforts to civilize the Salvadoran state without effecting major changes in the military sphere were doomed from the start. Salvadorans are fond of an old adage, "It is extremely easy to militarize a civilian, but practically impossible to civilize the military." By January 1980, the old guard of the military had regained control of the army and displaced the reform-oriented group. Working in tandem with the death-squads, the military stepped up the killings of suspected "communists"—leaders of the popular movement, the Church, the universities, and even the Christian Democrats. The objective was to crush the opposition movement and force the reformists out of the provisional government.

By March the political composition of the junta had radically altered. Guillermo Ungo and his social democrats led the first wave of resignations from the government in January. In February the country's attorney general, a Christian Democrat, was assassinated. When his party's leadership, headed by Napoleón Duarte, refused to condemn the armed forces for the genocidal repression, the progressive wing of the Christian Democratic party resigned from the junta as well as the party. In the meantime, the mass popular movement had gathered unprecedented steam. In January more than two hundred thousand people marched through the streets of the capital, protesting the official repression and demanding a radical revamping of the state. It was by far the largest political mobilization ever assembled in Salvadoran History.

By April the principal social and political opposition forces of the past twenty years had joined into a powerful center-left coalition, the Democratic Revolutionary Front (FDR). The FDR included the mass popular fronts of the left, now numbering hundreds of thousands of members, trade unions, professional organizations, small business groups, student associations, the two major universities, the social democratic MNR, and the Christian Democratic Popular Social Christian Movement. "We have exhausted all peaceful means," Enrique Alvarez Cordoba, the first president of the FDR, explained to a *Newsweek* interviewer. "Many of us who are in the Front have tried to win the structural changes that our country so badly needs by working with past governments. We came to the conclusion that a change at the very center of power was necessary."

Napoleón Duarte was called in to head the new civilian-military government. By entering into a coalition with the military and the United States, Napoleón Duarte and his Christian Democrats lost their historic opportunity to bring about democratic reformism in El Salvador. Estranged from the popular democratic movement, their traditional source of power, and constantly

19

distrusted—and hated—by the extreme right wing, the Christian Democrats would be condemned for the next decade to playing the democratic facade of the U.S. counterinsurgency project.

The Civil War

The civil war exploded in March when the new "centrist" junta moved against the "extremes." On the same day that the military announced the agrarian reform and the nationalization of foreign trade and banks, a state of siege outlawing all public political activities by the democratic opposition was also institutionalized.

The far right led by Roberto D'Aubuisson responded first with a coup attempt. Unable to overthrow the U.S.-imposed establishment, they concentrated on wiping out the entire opposition spectrum—political parties, trade unions, and the Catholic church itself. The onslaught culminated with the assassination of the Archbishop of San Salvador, Oscar Romero, the sixteenth Catholic religious leader assassinated since 1977.

The bishop's assassination closed all political spaces. The opposition was forced to chose between exile and armed struggle. Thousands of peasants, students, and urban workers were willing to arm themselves and prepare for an insurrection. But the rapid flow of events and the terrible effectiveness of the state's death machine—army, security forces, and death squads—

gave the insurgents very little time for preparations. In addition, the revolution lacked the arms, the military expertise, and the unified political-military leadership capable of outwitting the will and power of the United States—the true power behind the ineffective Salvadoran army.

The founding of the Farabundo Martí Front for National Liberation (FMLN), the formal integration of all the left political-military organizations, did not occur until October 1980. The following month the entire leadership of the FDR was arrested and assassinated in San Salvador. By the time the FMLN launched its first military general offensive in January 1981, the huge mass movement supporting the revolution had been either decapitated or forced into exile. Observers estimate that between October 1979 and January 1981 some fifty thousand people were assassinated by the army, the security forces, and the death squads.

The January 1981 FMLN offensive guaranteed the survival of the revolutionary forces. The professionals, students, workers, and peasants who were not assassinated and who did not go into exile constituted the first units of what would soon grow into a formidable people's army. The FMLN began to build sanctuaries in the mountainous northern and eastern parts of the country, supported by a highly organized and extremely motivated peasantry. These were the campesinos who had toiled for a hundred years on the coffee, cotton, and sugar estates, the descendants of the victims of the 1932 genocide, the wives, children, and relatives of those dead and maimed in the last years of repression. The FMLN had become their army and their only hope.

From these human trenches, the FMLN successfully resisted wave after wave of massive "scorched earth" campaigns by the military, incursions designed to destroy all means of livelihood (crops, domestic animals, water supplies) in the zones of conflict in order to "drain the water" (the population) and "catch the fish" (the guerrilla), as preached by classical counterinsurgency manuals. Although thousands of refugees began pouring into the neighboring countries, Mexico, and eventually the United States, the revolutionary forces held their ground and began to "liberate" the zones by dismantling most of the government's fixed positions.

By the end of 1983 and the beginning of 1984, the FMLN had developed such military capability that it began to overrun the largest military installations in the countryside. In addition, Mexico and France had formally recognized the political representativeness of the FDR–FMLN alliance. The major international bodies, the United Nations, and the Movement of Non-Aligned Countries had gone on record condemning the gross human rights violations of the government and urging a negotiated political solution to the conflict.

The Duarte Solution Fails

But the 1984 situation was the exact reverse of that of 1980. Now that the democratic-revolutionary forces had achieved international recognition, consolidated their gains in the countryside, and built a regular army, they lacked an active political presence in the cities. The grass-roots movement of the 1970s had been virtually destroyed, and the leadership of the Democratic Revolutionary Front exiled.

What was even more threatening to the revolutionaries, the reformist political vacuum left in the urban areas was being filled by the presidential bid of Napoleón Duarte. Duarte was campaigning against Roberto D'Aubuisson, the charismatic candidate of ARENA, the party of the agro-export sector. Duarte's electoral bid could not fail. He was receiving full political and financial backing from the United States. His carefully cultivated image of civic moderation was given an almost angelic light when cast between two "diabolic personae"—D'Aubuisson on the right and the "communist" revolutionaries in the hills. His platform promised heaven on earth: full implementation of the reformist packaged decreed in 1980, final democratization of the country, and a peace plan to reintegrate the rebels to political life.

In the United States, Duarte's 1984 electoral victory over "rebels and rightist" was presented as the crowning success of U.S. policy. The U.S.-

sponsored "revolution" was now "democratically" legitimated by a reformist political "center" firmly in control of the state apparatus and the military. In addition, Duarte's victory ended the international isolation of the Salvadoran government and built a bipartisan consensus in the Congress. Without any powerful opposition at home, U.S. aid began to flow at the rate of more than $1 million a day, the military received a fleet of numerous bombers and nearly one hundred helicopters, and hundreds of U.S. military advisors were now free to operate in the country.

In El Salvador, Duarte's promises of peace, social justice, and national reconciliation were winning his Christian Democrats a social base among the middle and popular classes. The support of these social groups, in addition to that of the U.S.-financed sector of the trade union movement, constituted a national mandate for the construction of a new political project. The battle for El Salvador appeared won. U.S and Salvadoran strategists began to predict that by 1986 the rebels would be reduced to the northern fringes of the country—the least populated and least economically important region. Both the extreme right and left, thought U.S. planners, would soon be forced to accept the success of "a centrist and democratic" U.S. "nation-building" enterprise.

But Duarte's U.S.-sponsored project did not turn out to be the proverbial light at the end of the tunnel. Duarte talked eloquently, especially to U.S. audiences, about democracy and reforms but proved incapable of subduing the military, whose sole concern centered on the war effort and the future of their institution. Despite superficial attempts at reform, the war component of the U.S. policy ended up deepening the structural polarization existing in Salvadoran society.

By the end of 1989 there was no room for political centers. Both poles of the equation, ARENA and the military and the FMLN, were feeding off the fires of a generalized state of war. After mastering the game of electoral politics amid a war-torn society, ARENA had come to control all three branches of government and begun to undo Duarte's structural reforms.

On the other end of the spectrum, by 1985 the FMLN had rearranged its forces in small units and spread them throughout the entire country. Soon new guerrilla bases would be springing up in twelve of the fourteen provinces, more local landowners would be paying war taxes and higher wages to their farmhands, and new recruits would be joining the ranks of the insurgency. By 1987 the combination of nationwide traffic stoppages, far more effective sabotage campaigns against the economy, and literally thousands of small, lighting ambushes on government forces were creating havoc in the military and the regime. The dramatic growth of the rebel forces and their military capability was demonstrated in November 1989, when the FMLN launched the largest and most effective campaign of the war. The rebels successfully moved the war to the principal cities, particularly San Salvador, and in the process managed to demonstrate both the military incompetence of the armed forces and their systemic brutality.

ARENA: The Party of an Oligarchy at War

In 1980–81 the days of the Salvadoran oligarchic state seemed numbered. The projects espoused by the rebels, on the one hand, and the United States, on the other, represented either the absolute or partial displacement of the oligarchy from the spheres of economic and political power.

Facing the most serious threat of its history, the Salvadoran oligarchy struck back. As already mentioned, the oligarchy ordered the assassination of some fifty thousand peasants, workers, and other civilians. As in 1932, the oligarchy resorted to the only solution it knew: the tactics of "total war." And in order to create a viable political formation that could compete with Duarte's Christian Democrats and eventually displace them from the U.S. counterinsurgency project, they founded ARENA in September 1981.

Roberto D'Aubuisson played the pivotal role in both efforts with the total backing of the most reactionary members of the oligarchy. D'Aubuisson, the exleader of ORDEN and the former director of ANSESAL, the infamous armed forces intelligence agency, had become the most powerful and astute politician of the Salvadoran right. Only the enormous weight of the U.S. government

and press would keep D'Aubuisson away from the presidency.

Duarte's electoral victories of 1984 and 1985 forced ARENA to recognize the nature and limitations of the new state imposed by the U.S. counterinsurgency requirements. As the principal executors of U.S. policy, the military were the "untouchables" and the supreme force. They stood well above the political parties and had veto power over all vital matters—political and economic projects to be implemented, the budget, and the key question of peace and war. The political parties could compete through elections for control of the state apparatus—the three branches of government. Coups and other traditional means of seizing state power were now strictly forbidden; they would only alienate the North Americans and unite the opposition around the FMLN. And without North American aid to sustain the economy and the war against the FMLN, the state would simply collapse.

In order to legitimate their party within the new state model, ARENA strategists adopted the rules of the electoral game and embarked on a two-track approach: they set out to break Duarte's political backbone while preparing the conditions to become the undisputed leaders of the loyal opposition.

By 1986, the deepening war, a catastrophic earthquake and a severe drought that crippled exports provided the golden opportunity ARENA sought. When the war economy began to touch

23

bottom, forcing the government to announce plans for imposing International Monetary Fund–style austerity measures and raising a war tax on capital, ARENA's friends in the National Association of Private Enterprise (ANEP) and the Chamber of Commerce retaliated. They called an economic strike against the government and in a matter of hours had shut off the entire country. By asserting its real power through its economic-political institutions, ARENA demonstrated the lame-duck nature of the official party and wiped out what little public confidence remained in the Duarte project. The road was thus paved for seizing control of the Assembly and presidency through the elections of 1988 and 1989, respectively.

By 1988, ARENA's leadership had mastered the art of electoral politics permitted in El Salvador. Its leadership understood that elections are won by the richest campaign chest, the magic of image-making in the high-tech media, the careful avoidance of controversial issues, and concentrating on and exaggerating to the utmost the defects and weaknesses of political opponents.

Accordingly, the party had ANEP and the Chamber of Commerce raise millions of dollars for their campaign chest, hired expensive campaign and media experts from the United States, and chose as their presidential candidate not the U.S.-discredited D'Aubuisson, but Alfredo Cristiani. Cristiani is a handsome, mild-mannered, soft-spoken graduate of Washington's own Georgetown University. Having struck in this manner a pact with the modernizing sector of the oligarchy—of which Cristiani is a chief representative—the party focused its political campaign on Napoleón Duarte's weaknesses and limitations: his incapacity to win the war, his economic incompetence, his party's incredible graft and corruption.

Central to ARENA's political strategy also was the careful cultivation of the military. Of strategic importance was winning over the support of Roberto D'Aubuisson's graduating class of '66, known as La Tandona ("the large class"), by far the largest and most powerful military clique in the country's history. The delicate political work was carried out by retired military men within the party's key leadership, such as D'Aubuisson himself and Colonel Sigifredo Ochoa. Furthermore, the party's strident anticommunism and nationalism as well as its promise to put the state apparatus at the disposal of a "total war" effort—one that would not distinguish between rebels and the civilian population—made ARENA the natural choice of the military. After all, the military had been extremely critical of the conduct of the war under the Christian Democrats and the U.S. "low intensity conflict" approach because these tactics, in their opinion, imposed too many "unnecessary limitations" on military activities, such as having to respect the human and political rights of the civilian opposition.

The Present

In the 1988 elections ARENA captured a majority of municipalities and Assembly seats. And with war raging in twelve of the country's fourteen provinces and with 64.2 percent of the eligible voting population abstaining, Cristiani captured the presidency in the elections of March 19, 1989. But instead of ratifying a clear national mandate and facilitating the formation of a new consensus around a right-wing project, ARENA's victory brought the country's state of war and social polarization to a head.

ARENA's economic policies began to roll back the clock and undo the moderate economic and political changes made by the previous government. The reprivatization of banks and foreign trade got underway. "Austerity measures" benefiting the richest 2 percent of the population were passed. The Supreme Court began to rule in favor of landowners whose lands had been previously expropriated in agrarian reform decisions affecting thousands of peasant families. And the ARENA-controlled legislature sought to pass "antiterrorist" legislation, which amounted to the institutionalization of a police state.

Dissatisfied members of the modernizing oligarchy and the middle class, Christian Democrats, social democrats, and a rising popular movement began to establish points of common agreement over the government's repressive and exclusive policies. ARENA's unwillingness to end the war by means of a political settlement also became a rallying point and organizing issue. The Catholic church–sponsored Permanent Committee for the National Debate, which comprises over seventy-four organizations ranging from small business sectors to trade unions and claims to represent over a million people, is a dramatic expression of the growing opposition that began to coalesce in 1989. However, the state of generalized repression and escalation of human rights abuses that accompanied ARENA's rise to power had effectively closed the narrow political spaces opened during Duarte's administration. By equating the struggle for economic and political rights with rebel support, the ARENA-military establishment had effectively canceled out all democratic political activities.

Local and international pressures forced the Cristiani government to pursue a "peace" policy, which consisted of a series of meetings with the rebels in Mexico City and San José, Costa Rica. But dialogue soon came to an impasse when the rebels made concrete proposals demanding the democratization of society and the strict observance of human rights as a precondition for their demobilization, and the government, cued by the military, kept demanding a rebel surrender. After the October 1989 meeting in Costa Rica, it became evident to the rebels that both the military and ARENA were just buying time to pursue their traditional objectives of using the war as an excuse to outlaw all political opposition while

25

pursuing an escalation of military activities.

After a trade union hall was bombed at lunch time killing and wounding dozens of leftist activists, the FMLN launched a military offensive "to unclog"—in the words of their leaders—"the impasse at the table of negotiations." The military strength demonstrated by the rebels in a push that took them to the heart of the principal cities as well as the army's incompetence and brutality, which culminated with the assassination in cold blood of six Jesuits and two women of Central American University, constituted a turning point of the war. Washington and a majority of Salvadoran businessmen—all of them former advocates of a military solution—came out of the November debacle convinced that neither side could win a military victory and that it was time to end the war through political agreements.

The FMLN Peace Strategy

The November offensive succeeded in demonstrating not only that the FMLN was deadly serious about ending the war through political negotiations, but that the insurgency was so mature and so powerful that it could use its military instrument to fulfill concrete political objectives: the FMLN pushed the country's leading forces into accepting the necessity of a negotiated political solution. In this manner, the FMLN successfully broke the negotiations impasse of the previous year and set a perfect stage for pressing for the democratization and demilitarization of the Salvadoran state, the principal objectives of its strategy. The agreement to resume peace talks signed in Geneva, on April 4, 1990—by far the most serious, binding, and comprehensive step toward peace ever taken by both sides—faithfully reflects the FMLN objectives at this time.

The document gives the U.N. secretary general an active and permanent role in the negotiations. It wisely sets first a preliminary period for reaching political agreements and a subsequent stage for agreeing upon a cease-fire, provided the human rights of the civilian population are being universally respected. The agreement also gives other Salvadoran social and political forces a vital part in the negotiations, thus involving in the decision-making process the entire national spectrum. Giving a central role to the world's most respected and most experienced negotiating body, the United Nations, actively involving all social and political forces in El Salvador so that a national consensus might emerge out of the negotiating process, and a logic demanding political agreements as a precondition for any demobilization—all these key concepts reflect the essence of the FMLN's conception of political pacification.

The FMLN believes that most social and political forces are ready to be mobilized in a national project involving the transformation and adaptation of the Salvadoran state to the radically new demands of a peace and democracy mandate. With the exception of the military elites and the most extremist members of the ultra-right, there is universal agreement that the state's structures shaped by fifty years of militarization and a decade of counterinsurgency war against its own population must change. Most forces also agree with the FMLN that if the rebels were to disarm and remove their military pressure without first setting in motion substantial reforms in the state's military and political structures and without guaranteeing the democratization and demilitarization of the state, the social, political, and military expressions of the conflict would go on indefinitely.

Similarly, for a cessation of hostilities to be fully binding, all acts of war must cease, both those acts carried out by the military state against civilian society—military operations as well as gross violations of the population's human and political rights—as well as those carried out by the insurgency. A cease-fire must be carried out within the context of political agreements that guarantee the democratization of society and full respect for the human and political rights of the population. Important agreements would deal with the size and social role of the military, the judiciary, and all laws governing elections and political life. For the FMLN is literally dying to leave behind the armed phase of its struggle and concentrate all its power and energies on a fair, democratic, and constructive political struggle with other forces in El Salvador.

The FMLN began to prove that it had become the Salvadoran force most attuned to the new national and international reality in January 1989.

At this time it offered to participate in the next round of presidential elections and abide by their results if the government ended its state of official repression and implemented the most basic democratization of the political structures. Behind these dramatic proposals were two realizations: that the Salvadoran conflict could not be resolved through military means alone and that, given the extent of the national polarization, a single force alone could not impose itself or its own ideological project on the rest of the political and social world.

The FMLN change of strategy had come solely on the basis of its own analysis of Salvadoran and Central American reality and before the collapse of the socialist camp had become evident. Particularly after ARENA's seizure of the state apparatus and the political crisis that ensued, the FMLN began to seek the participation of other social and political forces toward the construction of a centrist, reformist model of the state— what it considered the first humanizing step in the country's social and political evolution.

Particularly in the aftermath of the November offensive, there were no doubts within the FMLN that only a democratic and pluralistic system could win peace and achieve the level of political stability necessary for the gigantic tasks of pacifying, democratizing, and reconstructing our country. The FMLN believes that this democratic and pluralistic system can produce a national consensus government capable of healing the wounds of centuries and leading the nation during the future storms.

Ideally, the actual process of negotiations, passing through a stage of free and fair elections, which can serve as a national referendum of the peace process, must naturally lead into a stage of national reconstitution—for the redefinition of the state's basic structures—and this phase in turn should take us into the stage of national reconstruction.

CONCLUSION

The 1980s have ushered in a new phase of political change throughout the world. A worldwide trend toward demilitarization with negotiations as the accepted means of resolving regional conflicts, an insistence on respect for human rights, and sweeping pressures for democratization have radically changed the political face of the planet and will inevitably affect positively the outcome of negotiations in El Salvador.

Among the most welcomed casualties from the Old World is the Cold War, whose ghouls and devils have been haunting for so long the mists of Foggy Bottom and those State Department specialists responsible for El Salvador policy. Now there is hope that the old "demonic" policy that made such a monstrosity as the Salvadoran armed forces attractive and made the FMLN the worst of all possible evils will be rescinded in favor of a more empirical approach to reality. The most recent example of this old morbid infatuation was given by present U.S. Ambassador

William Walker: weeks after the entire world had confirmed the hand of the military behind the assassinations of the Jesuit fathers last November, the U.S. ambassador kept blaming the FMLN for such a heinous act.

The changes in Eastern Europe along with the recent changes in FMLN strategy, which demonstrate an honest disposition to collaborate toward the construction of an economic and political model acceptable to the United States, ought to move policymakers toward a change of policy. The failure of U.S. policy in El Salvador has fundamentally resided in the mechanical implementation of a counterinsurgency approach that declares the armed forces—an authoritarian and antidemocratic institution, by definition—the principal guarantors and implementors of U.S. interests. One could argue that since 1980 U.S. policy has only been successful in its ability to engage all Salvadoran forces in the most destructive manner possible: it supported the Christian Democrats to justify politically the killing off of the FMLN.

Now the FMLN, Christian Democrats, social democrats, and even sectors from Mr. Cristiani's government say they are willing to engage in a serious process of negotiations, and now that U.S. security no longer appears to be at stake in El Salvador, perhaps the U.S. Congress and Bush administration can be convinced to try to engage all Salvadoran forces constructively in the pacification and reconstruction of their land.

The dismantling of the counterinsurgency war-state and the founding of a democratic, independent, and socially just nation-state constitutes the only national political project that can satisfy and unite the vast majority of Salvadorans. This is, in essence, the same political dream that inspired the liberal patriots who declared our independence from Spain in 1821. This is the same political project which motivated the formation of the National Opposition United (UNO) in the 1970s, and this should be the project to unite all Salvadorans tomorrow. Given our past experience we still have to ask ourselves and our North American friends, "How can the implementation of this American dream endanger the security and well-being of North Americans?"

1. Jenny Pearce, *Promised Land: Peasant Rebellion in Chalatenango, El Salvador*, London: Latin American Bureau, 1986, p. 351.

2. Ralph Lee Woodward, Jr., *Central America: A Nation Divided*, New York: Oxford University Press, 1985.

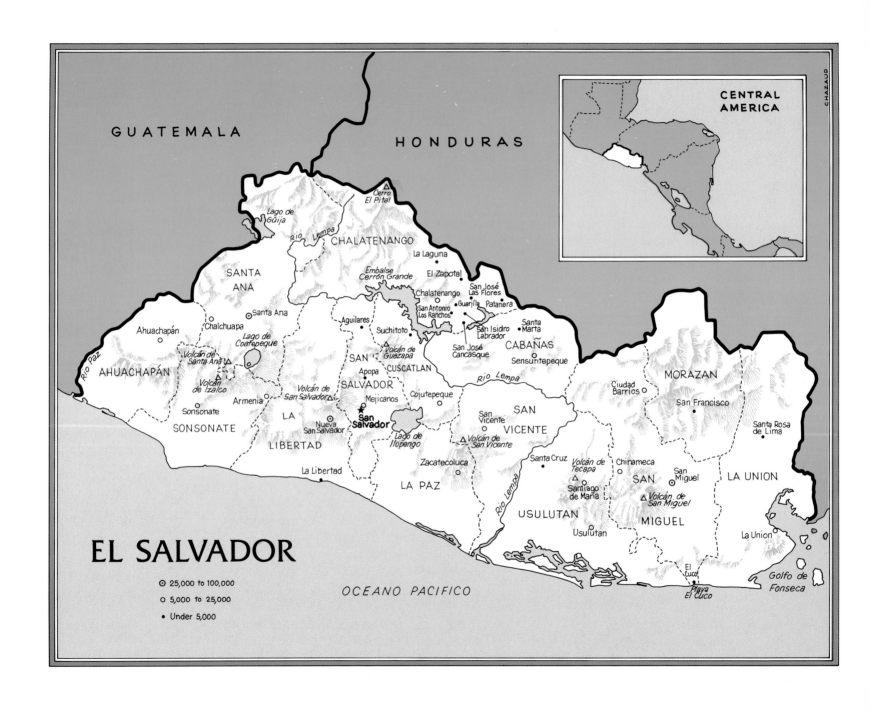

CENTRAL AMERICA

CHAZAUD

GUATEMALA

HONDURAS

Cerro
El Pital

Lago de
Güija

RIO   Lempa

CHALATENANGO

La Laguna

SANTA
ANA

Embalse
Cerrón Grande

El Zapotal

San José
Las Flores

Ahuachapán

Chalchuapa

Santa Ana

Chalatenango

Guarjila Patanera

San Antonio
Los Ranchos

Lago de
Coatepeque

Aguilares

Suchitoto

San José
Cancasque

San Isidro
Labrador

Santa
Marta

Volcán de
Santa Ana

Volcán de
Guazapa

SAN

CABAÑAS

Sensuntepeque

MORAZAN

RIO Paz

Volcán
de Izalco

AHUACHAPÁN

SAN
SALVADOR

Apopa

CUSCATLAN

Rio Lempa

Ciudad
Barrios

Armenia

Volcán de
San Salvador

Mejicanos

Cojutepeque

San Francisco

Sonsonate

San
Salvador

SAN

Santa Rosa
de Lima

SONSONATE

LA

Nueva
San Salvador

Lago de
Ilopango

San
Vicente

VICENTE

Volcán de
San Vicente

Chinameca

SAN

LIBERTAD

Santa Cruz

Volcán de
Tecapa

San
Miguel

LA UNION

La Libertad

Zacatecoluca

LA PAZ

Rio Lempa

Santiago
de María

MIGUEL

Volcán de
San Miguel

La Union

USULUTAN

Usulután

El
Cuco

Golfo de
Fonseca

OCEANO PACIFICO

Playa
El Cuco

EL SALVADOR

⊙ 25,000 to 100,000

○ 5,000 to 25,000

• Under 5,000

PHOTOGRAPHER'S NOTES

*F*or the first time in over a month of living in the mountains I was scared. Night had fallen and the people around me, normally relaxed and jovial, had turned dead serious. We had just gotten word that the Salvadoran army was making one of its periodic sweeps. It was time for us to move. This was another attempt by the army to "dry up the sea to catch the fish," and I was part of that sea.

The Salvadorans gave me a choice. I could stay where I was and hope that when the army found me they would just take me back to San Salvador and, after some questioning, send me on my way. Later my friends would do what they could to get my exposed film back to me. Or I could accompany the community I had been living with and take my chances with them. I opted for the latter. I was given several tortillas and told to make them last as long as I could. No one was sure when, or if, we would be able to stop and cook. I hid my film in the crevice of a stone wall, stuffed my hammock in my daypack, and fell in line. We couldn't talk or use flashlights, so I stumbled along the rocky path as best I could.

For ten days we walked and waited, and walked some more, circling the area to avoid meeting up with the army, often in pouring rain, always with little to eat. Whenever possible we slept in the shelter of abandoned and partially destroyed houses, but often trees and sheets of plastic were our only protection. Toward the end of the *guinda* (mass evacuations) we had to cut branches to camouflage ourselves while Huey helicopters flew over a ridge and A-37 jets dropped five hundred-pound bombs on Patenera, a small village we had left only a half hour earlier.

The people with whom I was fleeing were not armed guerrillas but campesinos, peasant farmers who for generations had scratched a living out of the rocky hills.

This odyssey began with an invitation in March 1985 to document the visit of the mayor of Berkeley, California, to that city's sister city in a rebel-controlled area of Chalatenango province. San Antonio Los Ranchos had been a farming community of several thousand inhabitants, reduced to a few hundred by five years of war.

It wasn't long before I realized I was witnessing something that belied the images of war and revolution that we get from the media. The reality was not that of backward peasants duped or forced into service by guerrillas taking orders from Moscow via Cuba. Rather what I saw was tightly knit communities made up of families, often quite religious, who were tired of watching their children die of malnutrition and of living in wrenching poverty. Because they had organized themselves to change this situation, they were being labeled subversives by the Salvadoran government and now had to use all their intelligence and creativity just to survive. Some were working in the fields, while other had to shoulder rifles—rifles that had been seized from the Salvadoran military, which had received them from the U.S. military. Others tried to teach, though with little formal education themselves. Others learned basic medical skills and walked the hills from community to community doing what they could to heal the wounds of war. Others dug bomb shelters or latrines. All in all, it didn't fit the propaganda. How could these people be a threat to the national security of the most powerful nation on earth?

I asked my host if I might be able to stay after Mayor Newport left. I wanted to go beyond the rhetoric and the flashy images of war. I wanted to show people back home the face of the "enemy." After all, if we as a nation were going to fund another war, we at least had the right, if not the obligation, to see who would be doing the dying. It wasn't our boys, but it was our dollars.

Life in the mountains was hard. The army's search and destroy operations had been partially successful, and many of the fruit trees had been cut down and fields burned. That left beans and tortillas, beans and tortillas three times a day, seven days a week. The constant overflights by re-

connaissance planes, followed by bombing and mortar attacks in the surrounding area, was unnerving at best. There were no phones, electricity, or running water. Communication with the world beyond the mountains took weeks; with home it was impossible.

We danced to local marimba bands, listened to the radio for news, and sang along with Madonna's "Material World," a big hit at the time even in the wartorn hills of Chalatenango. I dreamed of loved ones and pepperoni pizza. But I also made many friends, some of whom I would see again on future trips. I would find them in refugee camps on the outskirts of San Salvador in 1986 or in the Mesa Grande camp in Honduras in 1987. They had been captured by the army or driven out by the constant bombings, fleeing on foot through the mountains. Many of these campesinos later returned to Chalatenango, determined to rebuild their communities, where I met them again in 1988. There, they told me of others who had been captured and killed.

When finally there was a lull in military operations in the area, I was able to leave the mountains of Chalatenango, smuggled from family to family at great risk to them. I had lost twenty-five pounds, but I had gained something much greater. I had seen people of all ages maintain a sense of optimism, compassion, and humor in the face of incredible challenge and loss. But what was it that sustained these people through all these years of war? Was it just sheer determination and a refusal to accept poverty and brutality? Was it a love of life that they refused to let die? Was it a vision of a better life for their children and their children's children?

It was these and other questions that would draw me back to El Salvador seven more times over the next five years, the last being November 1989.

It was then that the Farabundo Marti National Liberation Front (FMLN) launched its largest offensive of the ten-year-old war. Although both the Salvadoran military and the U.S. embassy knew of their approach, they were unable to prevent over two thousand armed guerrillas from entering San Salvador and over three thousand others from entering three other major cities.

It was not the fifty-six thousand Salvadoran ground troops that caused the guerrillas to withdraw but the air force's use of massive firepower and the disproportionate loss of civilian lives and destruction of their homes.

One evening, as a group of journalists either half-heartedly watched or tried to disregard the film *Platoon* as it played in the Camino Real Hotel, we were interrupted by the real horrors of war. From the hotel window we could see the Salvadoran air force rocket and strafe the Zacamil neighborhood for the second night in a row.

Their planes dropped Bengal lights, turning night into day. Helicopters hovered as their red tracer bullets streaked through the air, and white-yellow rockets tore through the night and exploded. It was almost beautiful. Except that on the receiving end were real people, not Hollywood extras.

The next day, the Escalon neighborhood, home to wealthiest of Salvadorans, with its manicured lawns, ten-foot-high walls, and armed guards, was under siege. FMLN guerrillas had penetrated the unpenetrable: the cradle of security and complacency. Not far away they were at the same time in the luxurious Sheraton Hotel.

The FMLN was making a point, or rather several. First, that the Salvadoran air force would employ a different military policy for the neighborhoods of the rich than for the poor. Unlike the poor barrios, they would not be victim to the wrath of jet bombers, helicopters, or the C-47 planes that fire 4,500 fierce 60 caliber bullets a minute. Second, that if the FMLN could enter these wealthy neighborhoods and spend the night in those very homes, as several dozen did, they could go anywhere.

Ten years of training and arming the Salvadoran military have done nothing to end the war. The real causes of the conflict—extreme poverty and a lack of human and political rights—have not been addressed. Similarly, the policy of placing strategies for war over negotiations or genuine solutions to El Salvador's problems has gone nowhere. But there has been a high cost: $4 billion in U.S. tax dollars, a million and a half Salvadorans driven from their homes and seventy-four thousand dead. There will never be light at the end of the tunnel as long as an antiquated Cold War mentality continues to govern U.S. foreign policy toward Latin America.

33

DAY

TO

DAY

Making tortillas, Los Amates, Chalatenango province. Corn tortillas and beans remain the staple for the urban and rural poor in most of Central America.

This is my country,
land of ancestors and deer,
of volcanoes and lakes, and
sisters barely five years old
        who already dream of becoming mothers.
Cradle of grandchildren.   Country where women
                repose
after loving and painful childbirth.
Country of naked bodies dumped in the streets.
Dark corner
where people do not ask for
permission to weep,
much less for sympathy
or pity.
Country of flowers.
Country of children afoot in the hills.
Country of smoke,
of planes overhead, of
armed men.
Country consumed by centuries.
Desolated and plundered.
Country of rivers that flow down to the sea
and of roads that climb the mountains.
Country of outlaws and
patriot-executioners.
Country nourished with its own blood.
Country of dreams.
Where hope is silent and
gradual as an awakening.   Sure
as a cat in the night.
Our country which is in heaven
but grows on earth.

Country making its painful way.
Emerging from dens and lairs.
Ancient phoenix.
Big as a tall tale.
Devastating country
of dreams never realized.
Child-country.   Casket for the dead.
Strong-box country.
Famous and infamous.   Precious
        as the fingers of your hand.
Infant-country that grows like a clambering vine
and does not deserve to die.
Old in its ways,
        and listening to no one.
Importer-exporter country.   Shattered country.
Stinking of military advice.
Country where international business sticks
its fingers
        and daggers
                and bullets
                        and lies
with the awful thrust of its economic power.
Country of birds and orchards.   Iguana country.
With lily-shaped lagoons and volcanoes like
                glowing lamps.
Patience burgeons in your brow and
determination in your hands.
And though your face betrays grief,
the spirit is there in your eyes and
your hair is a storm.

Those who feel free of sin
have cast the first stone
and wait to cast the last,
preachers with white necks
and gold-handled pistols.
Country small
as silence.   Timeless as love.
Delicate as the damp mouth that
envelops the hard and trembling body.
Our country, clawed by foreign hands
trying to snatch it up.
Infant at the breast of its terrible history.
Country in the trauma of liberation, reeling
with the madness of incendiary ideas.

We are beginning to know you.   Magical country.
Inexplicable country.   With all the faults
that jar and upset us.   Inextinguishable
and tireless country.
Like all the rivers of the world.   Cradle song.
Mother of illiterate heroes.
Father of children who eat honey
from the combs in their trees.
Mysterious and moving country.   Unhoped-for country.
Nest of quails and lair of thieves.
Country of everyone and no one.   Of the Nahuatl
and the Pipil.   The Christians and the West.
Universal and cosmic country.   Indian country.
Campesino country.
Real, unreal, visible and invisible.
My homeland.   My enemy and friend.

Planting peanuts near Aguilares, San Salvador province. The local campesinos' long history of support for Christian-based communities committed to social change has made them the target of frequent military and death-squad attacks for more than a decade.

6 a.m. Spinning hemp for rope, La Laguna, Chalatenango province. Since the late 1970s, La Laguna has been the scene of fierce fighting between government troops and FMLN rebel forces, but the town's residents try to retain a semblance of normality.

Sawing boards for house construction, near
Ahuachapán, Ahuachapán province.

Fishermen, Pacific Ocean, El Cuco, San Miguel province.

Children of displaced families fetching water, La Palma slums, San Salvador. More than half a million people have sought escape from the war in refugee camps or in ravines and hillsides around the capital, where they have subsisted for years without water, sanitary facilities, or electricity. Nationally, over 45 percent of the population does not have clean drinking water.

The crater rim of Lake Ilopango rises in the distance as a fisherman returns from a morning outing in the glistening waters. The lake, just outside San Salvador, is a popular weekend retreat for dwellers of the overcrowded capital city.

Day laborers planting corn near the foot of the San Salvador Volcano, on the road to Quetzaltepeque just outside El Salvador's capital. Land distribution is one of the country's most untractable problems, and still today just 2 percent of the population controls the best 60 percent of the arable land.

Campesino children in war zones, Chalatenango and San Vicente provinces. The nation's young are the prime victims of poverty, hunger, and war. Malnutrition and disease alone account for the deaths of one out of every four Salvadoran children before age five.

Shoeshine boy, San Salvador. Low wages and a long-standing unemployment rate of 50 percent forces many youngsters out of the schools in search of work.

Musicians take a break during National Association of Salvadoran Teachers (ANDES) rally, San Salvador.

Shelter of tin, cardboard, and plastic is home for this family at the edge of La Bermeja cemetery, San Salvador.

Men taken off bus for an ID check, on the road to Ahuachapán, Ahuachapán province, near the border with Guatemala. With the steady spread of rebel activity to all of El Salvador's fourteen provinces, heavy security measures now affect every corner of the country.

Street vendors, Santa Tecla, San Salvador province.

Young street vendor, San Salvador.

Military on patrol in the low-income Mejicanos neighborhood of metropolitan San Salvador. The district has long been a center of political organizing.

Soldiers in camouflaged gear have become everyday sights in Mejicanos, where some of the Salvadoran capital's poorest residents have often clashed with government security forces.

Watching the exhumation of two unionists,
the boy covers his face in an attempt to mask the
smell of death.

The bodies of two unionists, one a leader of the National Association of Salvadoran Teachers (ANDES) the other from the Unified Federation of Salvadoran Unions (FUSS), are exhumed. Both had been taken prisoner by members of the military. Autopsies revealed that they had been tortured and then shot. Soyapango, San Salvador province.

Bodega No. 5, a banana warehouse in San Salvador.

Bodega No. 5.

58

Selling images of saints and spirits, Calvario Market, San Salvador.

The tattered shreds of clothing enable this woman to identify the remains of her son, a death-squad victim missing for six years. El Pozo de la Muerte ("The Well of Death"), Armenia, Sonsonate province.

Waiting for customers, Cuartel Market,
San Salvador.

San Salvador bus.

Vendors receiving their copies of *El Mundo*, San Salvador's afternoon daily. Although there is no official censorship, the threat of death-squad violence results in a virtual ban on serious political debate in the nation's remaining three major dailies. The journalistic casualties have included two major opposition dailies—*La Cronica del Pueblo*, closed in 1980, and *El Independiente*, shut down in 1981.

Although they earn only two cents per paper sold, these men wait patiently to see if there will be more papers for them to sell.

With old Credence Clearwater Revival tunes blasting over a loudspeaker, a clerk pays a winner at one of dozens of well-patronized *lotería* gambling halls found in many of the country's towns and cities.

Making burlap bags at Sacos Cuscatlan, a union shop in San Salvador where eight union organizers were shot
and killed by authorities during a 1980 strike.

Shoemaking, a traditional local industry, San Salvador.

Near a military barracks, San Salvador.

A mother looks into the coffin of her slain son just before joining the funeral procession for him and three other young men killed by unidentified assassins as they returned home a day earlier in Apopa, not far from San Salvador. October 1988.

Lowering casket into common grave.

70   Annual Day of the Soldier parade, Military Academy, San Salvador.

The bodies of six members of the FMLN lie exposed in a corner of the cemetery in Chalatenango City, Chalatenango province. Earlier in the day a seventeen-hour battle had been fought as a result of a guerrilla attack on military headquarters there.

Religious worker, Madre de los Pobres, San Salvador. Threats, attacks, and assassinations have become commonplace for nuns, priests, and religious workers, labeled as subversives because of their work with the poor. Since 1977, eighteen religious workers, including Archbishop Oscar Romero, have been murdered.

In front of the military high command, San Salvador.

Ruben Dario office building in San Salvador, where 200 people died in the October 10, 1986 earthquake. Compounding the nation's profound misery, the massive quake severely damaged much of the city's central business area and ravaged slum areas swollen by the influx of refugees from the countryside, killing 1,500 and adding 200,000 people to the legions of the homeless.

Although El Salvador's government received massive foreign earthquake emergency aid, relief efforts were hampered by corruption and inefficiency, leaving to churches and individuals the formidable job of feeding and clothing victims, here reaching for corn proffered by a volunteer.

Gravesites in San Salvador's main cemetery, La Bermeja, become a playground for this young kite flyer. After the earthquake, the homeless settled in any open areas they could find, including this cemetery.

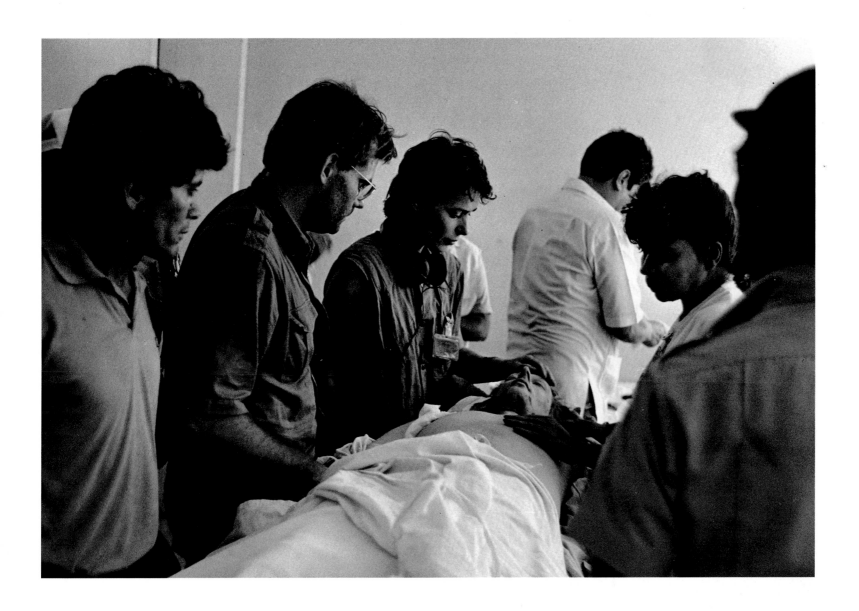

Dutch journalist Cornel Lagrouw lies dead in the Usulutan hospital, shot by government soldiers as he filmed the taking of the town of San Francisco Javier by FMLN guerrillas on election day. Two Salvadoran journalists also were killed by government forces as they covered the 1989 presidential elections.

Desks destroyed during the June 1980 army takeover. University of El Salvador.

Students study for exams behind doors painted with acronyms for the five organizations that make up the FMLN. "Together Until Final Victory." University of El Salvador.

Young man at graveside of his six-day-old daughter. La Bermeja cemetery, San Salvador.

Opposite: Civil Patrol headquarters, Mejicanos, San Salvador.

IN
THE
MOUNTAINS

Carrying food to FMLN camp. Unable to grow their own food, rebels must purchase their provisions at towns often hours away from their camps.

Someone is watching us.   Someone
whose touch
                slight
as a house cat,
envelops us
in gardens of dead flowers
and luminous reflections.   Someone comes
                and kisses
the foreheads of the compañeros.   And knows
we shall all meet in the crematory fire.
Someone knows that we must listen.   Someone
                unknown.

The strangers appears before us
with their immense comet tails of
                stars
                        streaming into the sea.
We realize they are made of fire.
Seething with life and death.

Someone who speaks like a child with hands
                of stone.
Strong hands that unleash furious things
and a voice full of terror and trouble.
Someone whose head teems with ideas.
Someone of a new generation
descended from the first signs of life
                on earth.
Master of his hands but not his tools.
Someone of centuries past
on the threshold of the future.   Someone
like leaves in the wind
announcing the coming storm.

Someone whose innocence assures us all
that our ideas are deep
                and simple.
Someone who sculpts bridges
and raises building that are like mountains.
Inconceivable highways.   Ravage of sorrow.
Man consecrated at others' expense.
World constructed on other worlds.
Someone who is our brother
                and also our enemy,
peering over a shrouded horizon.
Someone whose aspirations are comprised
of small realities and profound desires.
Someone like yourself,
who feeds and clothes the world
                and brings good fortune to others
while his own fortune
hangs   from tiered cells
                and wretched hovels.
Someone accustomed to vagrant sorrows,
who wonders
when they will cease.   Beautiful root
of the flourishing tree of contradictions.

Transporting supplies, northern Chalatenango province. Rebels enjoy much popular support in this
restive region and move about freely in small groups, while army troops must be ferried in by helicopters or
in truck convoys.

A girl and her yo-yo liven up a rest stop for an FMLN combatant.

Opposite: Rebel assault rifles offer a leaning post for youngster in Patanera, rural Chalatenango province. Rebels enjoy friendly relations with local youths, who often act as their messengers and lookouts.

Rebel couple waiting for breakfast, FMLN camp.

Morning drill, FMLN camp. Frequent drills assist rebels in maintaining discipline and combat readiness.

Guerrillas.

FMLN Comandante Lionel Gonzalez (left), gestures as fellow commanders Dimas Rodriguez and Facundo Guardado and unidentified combatant listen. The commanders' clothing, and the weapons of many of their forces, were seized from U.S.-supplied Salvadoran army units.

Guerrillas, young messengers pause for refreshments with local woman in La Laguna, Chalatenango province.

Grenade and comb. Zapotal, Chalatenango province.

94

Two guerrillas, San José Las Flores.

Opposite: Rebel soldier pauses to chat at San José Las Flores, Chalatenango province, while shopping for provisions for his unit, which operates in the region.

Bomb shelter near San Antonio Los Ranchos, Chalatenango province. Tunnels such as these offered refuge to families that refused to abandon their homes despite repeated bombings. During protracted military operations, people remained in the shelters for days. Unable to cook, they subsisted on sugar, cornmeal, and water.

School in war zone. El Tamarindo, Chalatenango province. Makeshift open-air classroom was destroyed during military sweep two weeks later.

Bombed houses. San Isidro Labrador, Chalatenango province. Most of the town's population fled to the cities or refugee camps in Honduras after frequent attacks by A-37 bombers and rocket assaults by OV-2 "push and pull" aircrafts, both once heavily used by U.S. forces in Vietnam.

San Isidro Labrador school destroyed in government bombings.

A letter from loved ones. Conacaste, Chalatenango province.

They observe you with their thoughts.
The working men.
They sleep tranquilly.
Nobly serene.   Their skin
flowing like your rivers and
their voice in the wind
                              and the trees.
Their eyes are like mine
and yours,
            seeking
not vengeance, but compensation.
In sunlight we are equally transparent,
shimmering like a country day
deliciously green in the rain.
We are the same,
approaching new horizons at the speed
                  of stars and doves
whose flight would span the universe.

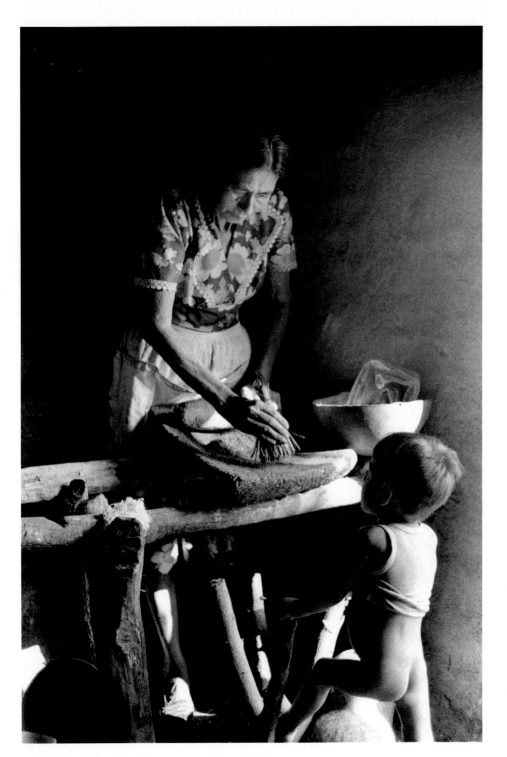

Grinding coffee. Dos Pinos, Chalatenango province.

Removing stitches from a shrapnel wound at community clinic. San Juan, Chalatenango province. The clinic itself, where civilians, FMLN combatants, and captured government soldiers were treated, was destroyed by bombs days later.

Fleeing the army near Los Amates, Chalatenango province. During military operations, entire communities leave their homes in *guindas*, or marches, to avoid contact with the army, which could mean interrogation, relocation, imprisonment, or even death. The walks can last from days to weeks. This group was on the eighth day of a ten-day *guinda*.

After a ten-day *guinda*, a local community representative in Los Planes, Chalatenango province, reads list of houses, livestock, and crops destroyed by the army.

REFUGEES
AND
THE
DISPLACED

Displaced campesinos gather in an abandoned schoolhouse after two weeks of fleeing an army operation. They described their odyssey to representatives of the Lutheran church and international human rights observers from Americas Watch. Santa Cruz, Usulutan province.

They want our lives to belong to them,
to the animals, the military I mean,
the "national" army.   Officers
bloated with fire and hatred.
We only ask for peace, and
for something
from you:
We want you to know
of the horrors that plague us.

We must not forget,
nor shall we forget
all of those who were kidnapped, who
are still today
              disappeared:
Maria Alvarado, Teresa Sanchez
        and her six small children,
Angela Merino and her four little boys,
and the babies still sucking their milk,
so delicate:
Isabel Sanchez and Orlando Chicas.
From that day, September 11, 1981,
at six o'clock in the morning when
the national army came,
we have had no peace.
The rest of the villagers fled to the
hills.   Hungry, cold, wretched
                              and alone.
They must have suffered, not knowing
we had managed to hide in the brush
below. Because we couldn't run.   We
couldn't make it up to the hills
with them.   Everybody agreed,
the young people should save themselves.
We're too old to be of use any more.

So they went off, the boys and girls,
sobbing because they left us
to the mercy of the national army.
If they wanted to kill us, let them kill us.
              God's will be done.
We stayed behind with the small children,
keeping an eye on them from a distance.
We couldn't carry them.
So we left them in a hut,
where we could watch over them
from the brush.
Especially the ones
who were too little
to walk
        or run.
We never imagined
        those animals
would harm them.

But they sprayed them with bullets, riddled them
with bullets.
Because they say we belong to an accursed race.
The accursed race of the poor.

              Yet we are of the same blood.
                The same misery. . . .

They carted off our corn
and stole our chickens.
They took everything we had in Achichilco
and Los Pozos.
They left us with nothing
but this anguish
and the passion of our outcry
reaching you with these words.
Asking you to intervene.   With your hearts,
not your rifles.   With your humanity
            and your will
to put an end to these crimes.

Mother and daughter. Santa Cruz.

Cooking beans in the communal kitchen. San Roque camp, San Salvador.

Making hammocks for sale, one of the few ways refugees can earn money. San Roque Camp.

A family's single-room living quarters. San Roque camp.

Children at San Roque refugee center.

Checking the list of displaced people eligible for food at church-run program, San Salvador. Aided by contributions and volunteers from the United States, the Catholic and Lutheran churches have provided extensive services to refugees and other displaced people.

Calle Real refugee camp outside San Salvador.

Mass. Calle Real camp. Music is a significant element of religious services among the campesinos.

Domas Maria refugee camp, San Salvador. Many families have lived in shelters such as these since the early 1980s.

Orphans in a church-run center in the provincial capital of La Libertad, La Libertad province. Between 60,000 and 75,000 children have been orphaned since 1980.

THE JOURNEY HOME

One of the many buses leaving Meas Grande refugee camp, Honduras, for El Salvador.

*F*or children, the years ahead glitter like stars,
almost visible.　　　Their dreams
　　　　　　　　　　　　no longer hopeless.
Things are better these days, especially
if we measure our era in terms of galactic years.
All of the effort of the past is justified
　　　　　　　by this awakening
of radiant thoughts and welcome feelings.
We can hardly sleep
　　　　　　　　reaching
to take the stars in our hands.　　　Eyes
open to a growing humanity.
Wings
　　　　expanding, lifting
　　　　　　　　　　　to a higher authority.
We live in an optimistic age.　　　An epoch
　　　of purifying fire.
The fire they send to strafe
and blacken,
we have dedicated to our cleansing,
discovering its new measure.
We have made ourselves masters of wealth
and wisdom, at the cost
of our lives.
Thoughts born of suffering
grow more beautiful each day.
So much strange joy suffusing our soil.
All this enters into the dream
　　　　　　　that transforms us,
that makes us different
from what we were in somber times.

We invite ourselves to a celebration of the future.
We gather at the festival of life.
The cloak of light rests on our shoulders now,
luminous with planetary energy.　　　The knowledge
　　　coursing through our rough-hewn hands
　　　and our weathered brow, is this:
We are the world's most ancient children.

Let everything be part of the spirit
that transforms us,
making us participants in this world.
Fathers, mothers,
　　　　　　　grandfathers,
　　　　　　　　　grandmothers
created this dream
more real
as we awaken to the day.

Mother and daughter. Mesa Grande.

Morning chores. Mesa Grande refugee camp, Honduras. Thousands of campesino families fled army sweeps in the early 1980s by crossing the frontier into neighboring Honduras, where eventually they were confined in United Nations–sponsored camps such as Mesa Grande, where more than 20,000 lived by 1987.

Loading a truck for the journey back to their homelands in El Salvador in a 1987 United Nations–escorted convoy. More than 4,000 of the camp's residents returned home to an uncertain future. Another 3,000 Mesa Grande refugees have returned home in subsequent repatriations.

Sixty-eight-year-old woman. Mesa Grande.

The journey home begins. Children as old as seven had never known life beyond the barbed wire fences surrounding Mesa Grande. Others remembered little of their homeland.

Members of the Christian Committee of the Displaced of El Salvador (CRIPDES) occupy the National Cathedral to protest the government's refusal to allow the returning refugees to stop in San Salvador before returning to their places of origin. The refugees had wanted to visit with relatives and friends, who had also fled the country-side years earlier.

In El Salvador, soldiers watch as a caravan of refugee buses pass through a bridge roadblock in Chalatenango province. The government admonished refugees not to return to their native lands in the war-torn region, but relented when the returnees insisted on going home rather than to refugee camps in El Salvador.

After the two-day trip, women and children rest in the shade. Guarjila. The returning refugees worked for days to reclaim from the tall grass and bushes what they could of the bombed out ruins of their former town.

Opposite: October 1987. Arriving home after seven years. Guarjila, Chalatenango province.

October 1987. A tired recent arrival. Santa Marta.

Opposite: In newly repopulated Santa Marta, Cabañas province, community workers distribute food
donated by church groups. It would be nearly six months before the rains softened the earth so they could
plant their first crops.

Returning refugees wait in a convent in Suchitoto, Cuscatlan province, for a boat to take them home to Copapayo, one of the three sites being repopulated by the Mesa Grande returnees.

Tortillas and music. Guarjila, Chalatenango province. Despite frequent military harassment, arrests of returnees, and army operations in which several have died, residents of the repopulated areas vow never to leave home again.

March 1988. Having lived in makeshift shelters for six months after coming home from Mesa Grande, Honduras, a Guarjila woman uses sticks, rocks, and mud to build the walls of what she hopes will be her permanent home.

In one of the most recent repopulations, seventy families returned from the Mesa Grande refugee camp on August 13, 1988. Teosinte, Chalatenango province.

IN
THE
STREETS

March to commemorate the fifth anniversary of the assassination of Archbishop Oscar Romero, March 24, 1985. The U.S. government has acknowledged that Salvadoran authorities are shielding from prosecution Romero's right-wing killers. Despite more than seventy-thousand deaths in the past decade, not a single Salvadoran officer or death-squad member has been convicted.

*T*hose who say that people are good
   and don't know why.
Those who love civilization
without boundaries
                  and who delight
in the advent of happiness.
Those who believe in science
                  and those who don't
because they are discovering
other worlds
and dimensions.
Those who live with boredom and loneliness,
         sustained by electronic mists.

They look at us with beautiful eyes,
hearts racing in the face of death.
Look, now.   It is possible to touch our common skin.
Tenuous, marvelous waves of the same heat
                        pour through us.
Soon we will tremble,
         united
against ridicule and disappointment.
The anguish of being builder and
         destroyer all at once.
Generous, voracious, we hardly realize.
We are the same,
the rich, the benefactor, the
         good.
We who have finally found a place
to rest our disasters.

Opposite: Images of Archbishop Romero.

Fifth anniversary march.

Mothers of the Disappeared.

Protesting the capture of six human rights workers, Mothers of the Disappeared occupy the National Cathedral. April 1986.

Hanging a banner.

Mother's Day march led by Mothers of the Disappeared.

Workers at candy factory flank blackboard outlining their demands for pay raises, two pairs of shoes per year, and a pledge of no retaliation. The strike was settled for a small pay hike and one pair of shoes a year.

Soldier stands guard in the front office of the IUSA textile factory as striking workers gather in the factory compound. Troops were called in after the workers walked off their jobs and occupied the factory when management and the Ministry of Labor refused to recognize their elected union leadership.

Strikers look from inside IUSA factory compound as army troops mass outside. The soldiers left moments later but returned shortly after 4 a.m. to seize the compound. Dozens of workers were injured or arrested, and four hundred were eventually fired.

Reinforcement troops arrive at IUSA factory occupied by defiant workers.

Member of the Christian Committee for the Displaced of El Salvador (CRIPDES) holds sign: "Destroyed by military." Campesinos from all over the country converged on San Salvador to protest wholesale destruction and human rights violations by military units. Adopting U.S. counterinsurgency methods, the Salvadoran military seek to deny guerrillas support by sweeping through civilian areas and rendering the countryside barren, a tactic known as "drying up the sea to catch the fish."

Union supporter posts a sign calling for May Day labor march. May 1, 1986.

Members of the National Association of Campesinos (ANC) putting up posters during May Day march.

Ski-masked demonstrator fuels flames on a tire barricade blocking downtown San Salvador traffic during protest. March 1988.

Opposite: Preparing to show outrage at the capture and beating of a major union leader in March 1988, demonstrator fills up a can with gas at a downtown San Salvador Texaco station.

Spray painter leaps down from a wall in San Salvador. He has written, "Yankee aggressor: Another Vietnam awaits you in El Salvador. FMLN."

Campesinos demanding better credit terms to buy seed and fertilizer join in 1986 May Day march by 100,000 workers, the largest gathering in El Salvador since the military fired on the funeral procession for Archbishop Romero six years earlier.

U.S. embassy, San Salvador, morning of May Day, March 1986.

On a maternity hospital rooftop, workers gaze silently as a military helicopter hovers over downtown
San Salvador on a surveillance mission.

THE
OFFENSIVE

A wounded government soldier is carried to safety. The Escalón neighborhood, San Salvador.

Strange things.   Odd happenings.   A blue sky
with no planes.   Birds that aren't poisoned to death.
Children that don't fall under machine-gun fire.
A national army that is not an army of occupation.
No one sobs in clandestine pain.
Young people don't have to hide from
disproportionate, technical, modern, cruel,
unusual death.   Brother embraces brother
and no one
dies betrayed
        by the simple expression
                of life
    and feeling.
People sing in the streets, celebrating
the truth they have finally encountered.
The smell of gunpowder is gone, and bodies
                shimmer
        like far-shining stars.
Death is as natural
as the birth
        of a flower
or the return of day.

Victory will belong to the rich in spirit
and defeat
to those impoverished on their golden beds.
We all have something to say
in this spirit of jubilation.
Death's horsemen
retreat to their shadow-chambers
and reflect on the immortality
        of the human spirit.

A guerrilla watches for planes above the town of Apopa, San Salvador province, November 1989.

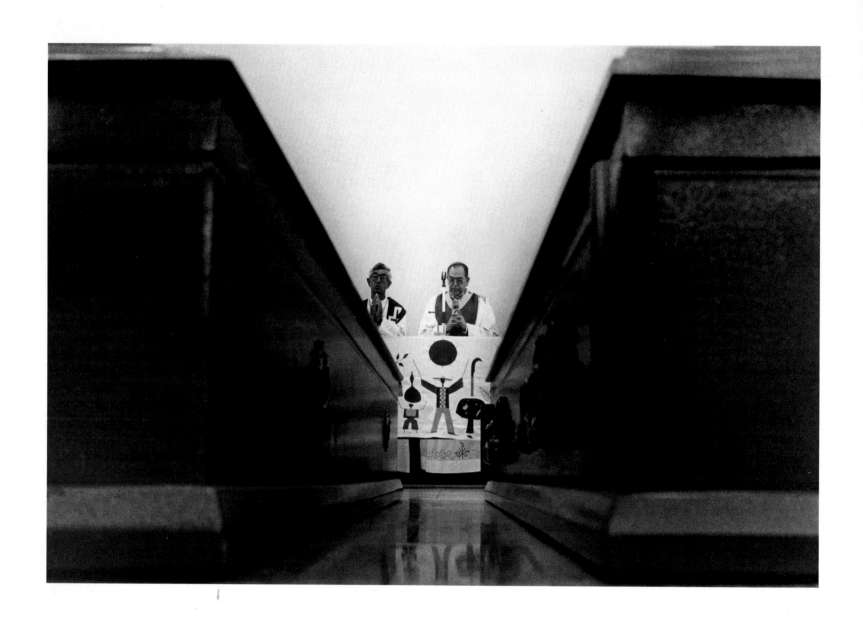

Archbishop of San Salvador, Monsignor Rivera y Damas, says mass for the six Jesuit priests, their cook, and her fifteen-year-old daughter, slain by government troops.

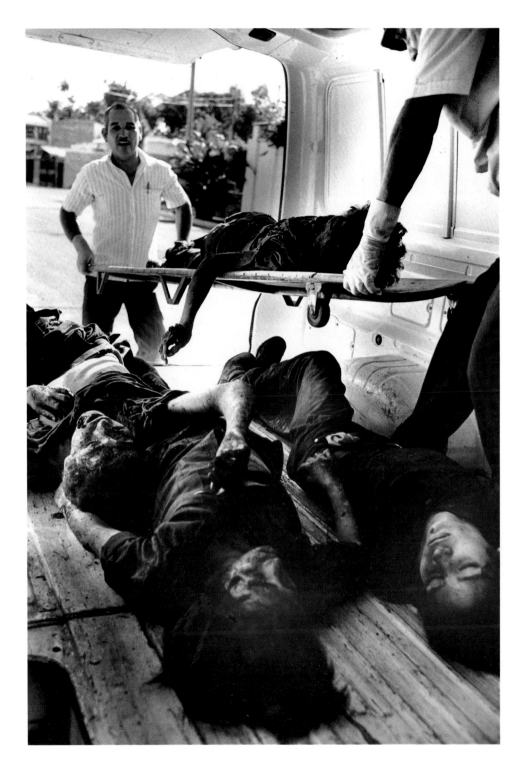

Killed in combat, guerrillas are loaded in a morgue
van. San Salvador.

With twelve Green Berets on the floor above, a rebel combatant maintains his position in San Salvador's Sheraton Hotel.

From behind a barricade a guerrilla speaks with local residents during a lull in the fighting.

Government forces in the San Benito neighborhood, San Salvador.

Under fire, members of El Salvador's Red Cross carry out a dead government soldier.

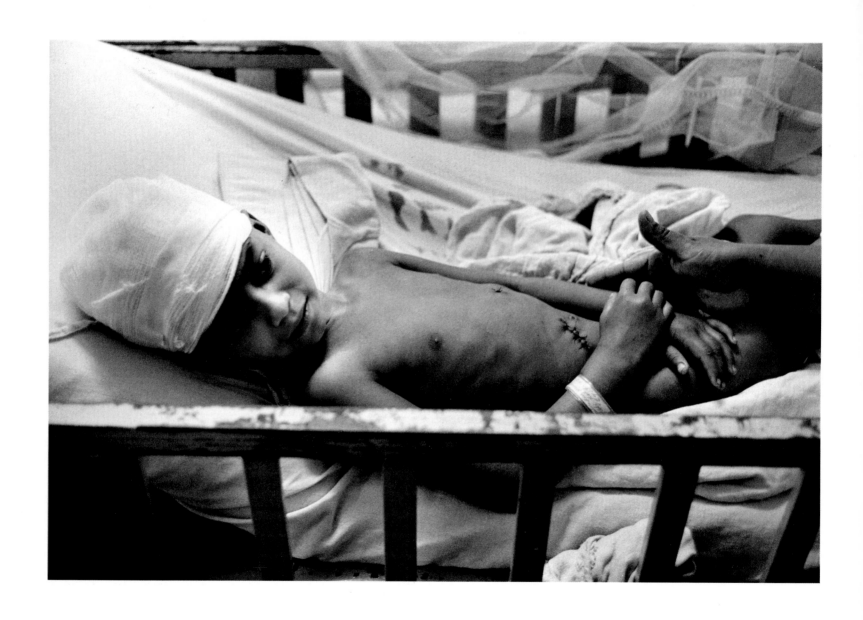

Wounded in the head by helicopter machine gun fire and in the stomach by rocket shrapnel, a young girl is comforted by a nurse. Benjamin Bloom Children's Hospital, San Salvador.

During the fighting in a wealthy neighborhood, one family's employee flees the area using his tee-shirt as a white flag to get through government lines.

With the help of the Green Cross, residents of Soyapango, San Salvador province, flee due to heavy fighting in the vicinity.

Red Cross workers are forced to hit the ground while attempting to evacuate one of the wounded during combat in Soyapango.

After using rocket-propelled grenades to dislodge rebels, government soldiers take a break.

Residents of Soyapango, San Salvador province, search the rubble caused by four bombs dropped in the area.

Due to the fighting, residents of the wealthy Escalon area of San Salvador leave their homes.

After six days of fighting, children of San Salvador's Zacamil neighborhood play with spent shells as a government soldier walks by.

ACKNOWLEDGMENTS

A book such as this can only be the product of the work and contributions of many. For me, before 1985 El Salvador consisted of dramatic images, horrifying headlines, and gut-wrenching testimonies from recently arrived refugees.

It was therefore with no small amount of trepidation that I left the familiar streets of San Francisco for the distant mountains of northern El Salvador. And it is there thanks should be given first. Maria and Evaristo welcomed me openly although I was a stranger. Their warmth, humor, and intelligence got me through unfamiliar and difficult times. I am also indebted to all those who opened their doors, shared what little food they had, and provided a place to hang my hammock or cleared a spot on their floor for me to sleep. To those who led me through the mountains and smuggled me in and out on more than one occasion I offer my gratitude: their acts of generosity were made at great personal risk. To Ruth and Susana, Sebastian, Eric, Jamie, Beto, Crecensio, to all the others who must remain nameless, to the living and to the dead, thank you for your friendship, sacrifice, knowledge shared, and patience.

In and around San Salvador many people took the time to explain the role of their organization and did whatever they could to make my work easier and more productive. From San Salvador to the far reaches of the country Leo was a great driver, fast talker, and good friend.

In the early stages Anne Walzer contributed her artist's vision in many ways, creating the initial design and helping to sequence the photos. Jane Norling always found the time to lend her sensitive eye to the difficult process of editing the photographs.

I owe a great debt to Manlio Argueta for his beautiful poetry, which painted images of his country that no photograph could. A special thanks must go to Jennifer Manriquez and Stacy Ross, who spent innumerable hours turning the translation of Manlio's poems into a labor of love. Kathleen Weaver and Dan Bellm contributed much in the early translation as well.

Bob Baldock helped in many ways, from facilitating my first contacts with W. W. Norton to introducing me to my agent, Felicia Eth. My thanks to Felicia for her patience, humor, and endless phone calls. Her support of this project went way beyond the call of duty. Jim Mairs, my editor at Norton, was a pleasure to work with. With his belief in the book and the power of photography, I couldn't have asked for more. Candace Maté's beautiful book design cannot go without special mention.

Fred Ritchin's comments and suggestions were extremely valuable. My visits with Ruth Lester from the International Center of Photography were both encouraging and helpful. I am also grateful to all the photographers who took the time to look at my work, lending invaluable insight: Richard Bermack, Frank Espada, Kim Komenich, Ken Light, Susan Meiselas, and Totoy Rocamora.

From the beginning of the project the help of Raul Ramirez of the San Francisco *Examiner* has been indispensable: he facilitated my trips, helped write the captions, and was a wonderful traveling companion. Phil Bronstein, also from the *Examiner*, assisted me in getting around El Salvador on more than one occasion. David Loeb and Dickie Magidoff both contributed many hours in numerous ways. Many individuals also contributed financially to help the project get off the ground. Thanks also to friend and doctor Marilyn Ancel for all she did.

Above all, I will be forever grateful to Marlene Tobias, who was there from the beginning. In addition to her constant artistic contributions, she gave hours and hours of help with the mundane tasks of creating a book. Her belief in the project was unflagging, as was her support and endurance during both the good and the difficult times.

To those I may have left out, I apologize. To all my friends in the Bay area and elsewhere who will no longer have to ask, "So when's the book coming out?" Thanks.